BNP

Best NEW Poets

2015

50 Poems from Emerging Writers

Guest Editor Tracy K. Smith

Series Editor Jazzy Danziger

This book was published in cooperation with *Meridian* (readmeridian.org), Samovar Press, and the University of Virginia Press.

For additional information, visit us at
bestnewpoets.org
twitter.com/BestNewPoets
facebook.com/BestNewPoets

Cover design by Atomicdust | atomicdust.com
Text set in Adobe Garamond Pro and Bodoni
Printed by Thomson-Shore, Dexter, Michigan

ISBN 13: 978-0-6924200-9-6
ISSN: 1554-7019

Contents

About *Best New Poets*

Welcome to *Best New Poets 2015*, our eleventh installment of fifty poems from emerging writers. In *Best New Poets*, the term "emerging writer" is defined as someone who has yet to publish a book-length collection of poetry. The goal of *Best New Poets* is to provide special encouragement and recognition to new poets, the many writing programs they attend, and the magazines that publish their work.

From February to April of 2015, *Best New Poets* accepted nominations from writing programs and magazines in the United States and Canada. Each magazine and program could nominate two writers, each of whom would be granted a free submission. For a small reading fee, writers who had not received nominations could submit two poems as part of our open competition, which ran from April 5 to May 25. Eligible poems were either published after April 15, 2014 or unpublished.

In all, we received 1,734 submissions for a total of roughly 3,468 poems. Four readers and the series editor blindly ranked these submissions, sending a few hundred selections to this year's guest editor, Tracy K. Smith, who chose the final fifty poems.

Introduction

TRACY K. SMITH
September 15, 2015
Princeton, New Jersey

I have found myself mightily heartened by the poems you are about to read. Their authors are described as "new poets," though their work is of a caliber I'd be more comfortable describing as ageless, unafraid to sing of the things that have always led poets to sing: desire, loss, shame, impermanence, beauty.

That's not to say I don't find myself in the presence of the New, for I very much do. But what characterizes the New here isn't, thankfully, trendiness or irony or selfie-esque narcissism. These poems aren't angling merely to surprise a reader with their novelty. They're doing diligent and oftentimes masterful work upon the age-old constants. They are asking language to become a means of psychic progress. They are trusting that music and image and breath might be enough to make the realities of 21st century life even just momentarily bearable.

Bearable, despite the death of Trayvon Martin and the history such hatred reanimates. Bearable, despite every death that rends our lives. Bearable, despite the ways we inevitably fail one another: parents, lovers, children, friends, our deepest selves. Bearable, despite nationhood and borders. Bearable, despite the violence we inflict. Bearable, despite the violence of rape. Bearable, despite the ways we have found to render one another invisible. Bearable, too, despite the way that joy can cripple us, can put us in mind of everything that might snatch it from us before we are willing to let it go.

Maybe one way these poems manage to console is by inviting us into the quietest encounter, into a space where one vulnerable person is talking to another, saying only the simplest, truest things:

What a bad year it's been. What a slow
wallow of a season.[1]

until three boys from town

took a quiet girl into
the belly of our field

and made her open up.[2]

I think people can't listen
to certain kinds of stories.[3]

you are an idler   some tiny thing
frantically waving its hands[4]

The bells of the neighborhood church keep
Pealing on without you & do not call you home.[5]

I will be talking to you
for a long time when you wake[6]

I'm just so tired. I love you all tender. Goodnight.[7]

[1] "Fallow"
[2] "Harvests"
[3] "What Happened"
[4] "From the Cabinet of Counterweights & Measures"
[5] "A Place Where There Isn't Any Trouble"
[6] "Not Spring"
[7] "Definitions of *Body*"

*The series editor wishes
to acknowledge*

Jeb Livingood

Caitlin Fitzpatrick

Courtney Flerlage

Caitlin Neely

Anne Pittman

Jason Coleman

Emily Grandstaff

Atomicdust

Lena Moses-Schmitt
The Gate

In the classifieds,
        a help-wanted ad for a farmhand declares

I must know the anatomy of a horse. Because I am desperate,
I say I do know the neck of a horse:
                        it resembles the gray sleeve

of the shirt he wore
        in the motel off 81, and how the sleeve turned

away, and the arm inside it, the arm inside it holding open
        the door for me, me already not knowing
                        what to say—

earlier, on the side of the road, a field of mares
                pressed up against a gate.

Their long heads bent to the earth, the earth
riddled with their suede questioning.

What is anatomy if not this muscular looking,
                        our actions turned inward to make the outside match?
        The organs planted
inside the body, the body oblivious
                as a fence

surrounding the horses
      gathered around feed in the field.

Has fear ever inhabited you
so completely the world becomes in its loveliness

        a composition
existing only for everyone else?

There are some words I cannot say
      because I can't imagine them.

Tell me we haven't ruined everything.

In my everyday carefulness,
I have worried only about death
        not life or how it begins:

the one poppy opening

red in the field near the fence,
      & the horse, with an eye buried
        on both sides of his face,

          not noticing
because he can't see straight ahead,

not at the flower, & not at the foal,
      throwing its small body against the gate.

J. Jerome Cruz
Saudades

When Maria shot her mother's gun / at the ocean, the Atlantic expressed /
its hurt in a cadenza of waves. / She waded through this pain / until her dress
was no longer diaphanous.

*

Prayer: run & gun like her mother / taught her. Then, mania dissipated. / At
church Maria only sang along / with hymns that sent ascension / or grace.
Once, in fifth grade, / she mucked up the sign her mother / hung in the
kitchen. *Too Much of a God / Thing Loses Its Novelty.*

*

She never liked Ohio. Make that living / at home. For the same reason she
didn't jive / with Miles Davis, terrifying movies, or anything / to do with
parachutes. Too much tension & / testament, attack & release. When she
caught / those old videos of Al Jolson in blackface / she felt the same anxiety
she carried in Cleveland / as well as shame that she married the two.

*

What's present, her second therapist / said, *is the wilderness.* So Maria blended /
skin with ink until her chest was blessed / with an armada of starlings. *Why
not, /* her mother asked, *finches or sassafras, / the sourness of oranges? Or even
a gazette of all / the men who've gotten into your pants? Not / every flower needs
pomp & circumstance. /* Maria laughed & laughed like when / she went

Splitsville with her first therapist. / Not because he resembled Tennessee /
Williams, but because she hated how he kept / saying they just had a couple
more steps / to go. In his office her feet always felt / so motley, so cold.

*

The last thing she did / before heading to the coast / was watch a Cavs
game / with her mother. One / of the announcers said: / *Love is hard to
guard against.* / Maria bounced out for / a cigarette & left before / the
second half ended. / Her mother found all / the baggage & wailed. / The
clothes never got / sent through the mail.

*

In dreams her father spoke / either in tongues or psalms / lost or
unattainable. When it rained / their record player burned / feral. *Don't front,*
her mother said, / *if the undertaker gives you the brush-off.* / Soft, off the
backboard, as her father / always taught. When scalpel sought / all that was
wrong with her / knee, her father told scouts / *What y'all are missing out on is
the intangibles.* / *Like last Easter Maria chased down ants* / *in our pantry with
a vacuum.* / In lieu of ashes they found it / kismet to rest his stuff in the
locations / he felt most blessed. When Maria played / her father's Strat for
the ocean / the Atlantic expressed its hurt / in a cadenza of waves.

Emily Vizzo

It was a miracle route everyone had been searching for and the story caused a sensation

I.

To catch a bear
during daylight hours

draw a simple line of sugar
rimming the os ilium.

Make that be the telephone line
you use to call the dead.

Your ancestors will still be Ohio
bound, grassing.

Give them overnight charlotte
w/ the good news of passage.

There are four ways to become an American citizen:

1. Be born here.
2. Marry an American.
3. Become an American soldier.
4. Secure the necessary documents, called "green," called "natural."

Though there is the fifth way, less advertised.

II.

Around me, desert.

An angled border fence splits the leather
elbow of this mountain.

Upon approach I am filmed
by a camera flock.

There is a man with a large dog.
He walks around my car

twice.

III.

To catch a bear
during daylight hours

draw a simple line of sugar
rimming the os ilium.

Make room for your body
on the ground.

When finally a black bear
comes for you,

consider sweetness—
oranges, whole milk, candy wrappers, nectarines.

Let your body be a mouthful.
Let the black bear be

an American black bear. Your sister
taxa. What he takes from you at this point

depends on his hunger.
His will might be simple.

A lob of fur, rank. Cinnamon
huge skull & molar.

There may be an archipelago
of sugar mouthing, faintly erotic.

Rumbled underfur.
You may be violently claimed.

Remember, it was you that hoped
to catch a bear.

You huckleberry. You chum
salmon. You apiary. You pistol, holstered.

IV.

Reasons why you did not catch the bear

1. Your line of sugar, though sweet, was not simple.
2. The meat cupping your os ilium, though luscious, was not savory.
3. Curettage made tender your feet, your heart.
4. The black bear was not in fact American. See also: *Apprehensions, San Diego Sector. Unaccompanied alien children. Fiscal year 2014, 875. Fiscal year 2015, 987.*

The poem's title comes from David McCullough's history of the Panama Canal, entitled *The Path Between the Seas*, published in 1977.

John McCarthy
Definitions of Body

Body 1. "Of Work": My mother did not—collected disability in the mail. The body is a paycheck inside an envelope held up to the light. 2. "Of Water": My mother was a river. Carried me into a gulf. When I was thirteen I dove into the trashcan to find the sunken orange bottles that resurfaced among eggshells and coffee grounds. She pulled herself under her own current. 3. "Of Bones": Her skull was a bag of voices. When she breathed, her ribcage moved like fingertips tapping together. Her teeth turned yellow, then white, then ghosts. She swallowed her ghosts, until she filled up with too many. 4. "Of Christ": Has risen. Revived at the hospital. The blood put back into her body with blood. The way I stood in the dark room and touched the IV hole to make sure she was real. 5. "Of Lies": Erased. She is not real. She has the intention to be a wraith. When she wakes and I ask how she is, my mother looks past me. 6. "Of Proof": The note I found which read, *I'm just so tired. I love you all tender. Goodnight.*

Kara Kai Wang

Idiom

My father arrives in America in 1979 and takes a taxi to his new
apartment, three miles from work. His first night in San Jose, he meets
his landlady upstairs, who introduces him to her toothless cat. The
woman pronounces his name wrong and my father is too polite to
correct her. My father's name is Tian Fang which translates to a place in
the heavens, an island in the clouds. Every cloud, a silver lining.[1] My
father is a pear man and a diligent man. His first month in America,
he eats a pear with every meal, rinsing the fruit in warm water before
skinning it. He thinks the pears will help cure his headaches. The corner
market sells yellow Bartletts for a dime a dozen,[2] though the grocer, a
gray-haired Cantonese woman, tells him to try lighting incense instead.
The ghosts, she says, will leave you at the first sight of smoke. But
America and my father do not believe in ghosts. They believe in picking
yourself up by the bootstraps.[3] My father practices his English and buys
two radios for his one-bedroom apartment. His boss likes him because
he works through lunch. He will do this for sixteen more years. When
the first phantom tiger finds my father, he will close his eyes and tell
himself to buck up,[4] there are no such things as ghosts. My father will

spend his last failing years shooting phantom beasts as they appear. His

doctor will believe there is nothing my father needs. No mention of the

headaches, their growing frequency. None of us will know, my mother,

my brother, or me. This is no one's fault. My father's phantoms, all of

us. Even now, I am not sure who died and why. My father's handbook

of English idioms refers to this as a blessing in disguise.[5]

[1] 每一個雲一線希望
[2] 多如牛毛
[3] 採摘自己了由白手起家
[4] 扣下來
[5] 因禍得福

Leila Chatti

What Do Arabs Think of Ghosts?

I think the woman means *Muslims*—ghost
of a word mixed up with our bodies, as if they were
the same thing—but either way I have no answer.
I haven't asked around. There is too much
death—it swells our tongues. It chokes.
The soul is a bird flying; it doesn't rest long
and its language is different. There are three
nightjars preening under the evening's cloak,
by which I mean three souls. Are souls clean?
Are ghosts? If every sad death made
a phantom, my country would be thick with them,
we would breathe them like air, they would keep us living.
What do ghosts think of Arabs, I want to know—
our fires blooming like native blossoms, bombs
planted like bulbs awaiting the spring?
Death grows here. There are more every day.
Before she died, my grandmother could
only say her name. I don't know the names
of the dead accumulating like snowflakes, so many
the news talks about them as if they are one thing,
a mound of indistinguishable parts. Who
calls for them, who houses them in their mouths?
In skies blue as a door, the metal ghosts soar:
they have wings but are no bird, have no soul.
We know this better than anyone.

NOMINATED BY NORTH CAROLINA STATE UNIVERSITY

Lisa Dordal

Pretty Moon

Pretty moon, everyone said.
Before the noise, before
the fire. Two cars
and the cornfields idle
on either side. Like the eggs

of monkfish, emerging
a million at a time, knitted
into a gauzy shroud,
forty feet long, buoyant,
built for dispersal—the veil
between us and them,

thin. My cousin,
beautiful at sixteen,
dead at seventeen.
Pretty, pretty moon.
And me, at five, mouth open
not to a scream or even
to a word. Just taking in air,
quietly as a spider
entering a room.

Alysia Nicole Harris

Crow's Sugar

I stole a watermelon from your kitchen. I must have been about 18.
I'm thinking of a black-eyed angel.

The other boys said you wasn't worth your salt if you wasn't tasting me.
I hid my virginity under my shirt. And that summer we sang

like we had azaleas bottlenecked in our throats
when we'd catch a storm from the porch, our laundry swung on the
    muscular thunder.

A piece of me is corroded.
Rigor or love in our small fingers—a sweet sort of choking.

The squash, the corn, all sweeter than antifreeze—I must have been about 18.
I was full of your seed, and the lavender came down like a motorcade.

That summer was the summer God told me stars used to be audible.
Does it have to be a full six octaves of guns between us?

A piece of me is corroded. Is submerged.

Stars hit high notes. Ella and everybody up there,
throwing our heads back, letting the howl bloom upright—

They told me to drown your name in the second and third chorus of Ave Maria.
Nobody told me to call the crows Sugar.

I must have been about 18.
Back pew bridge to sorrow, wailing

if you wasn't tasting me on clean linen on newly tarred roads
if you wasn't teasing me out on a string.

Ella and everybody up there wailing, *I'm thinking of a black-eyed angel,*
the dope boy in the attic. Marry me! I am full of your seed.

Once I stole a watermelon from your kitchen.
You poured salt on and ate to the rind.

A piece of me is corroded. Leaves a stain
of beets between my lips sweeter than antifreeze on newly tarred roads,

the lavender came down like a motorcade in spring.

My body was a carcass. You poured salt on
and ate to the rind. But wasn't there syrup once?

Wasn't it sound, rigor or love? In our small hands
crickets shuck the night & leave their skin.

My body was a carcass. Ella and everybody up there wailing.
A sweet sort of choking.

I'm thinking of a black-eyed angel, the dope boy in the attic

innocent as Anne, as a wolf under the moon. Stars hit high notes.
A full six octaves of guns. Wasn't it sound?

I hid my virginity under my shirt. A stain of beets on our laundry
after we went hunting with revolvers, kneading the dead through soil.

Sweeter than antifreeze. I am
full of your seed.

I must have been about 24.
Nobody told me to call the crows Sugar.

This summer a whale, finchlike, eats from the uncoiled knot of my hand.

Nikki Zielinski

Midnight, Troy

Wine, rich & red. Drinking straight from the cask.
Her body below me in the grain we'd rationed

for a decade, how every place I buried
my face smelled of baking bread. Their thrill,

the children, when we opened the gates—the fields beyond
they'd only ever known by the sounds of siege & slaughter—

& the perfect polish of that horse, the enemy's artistry

evident in every carved hoof. Everyone agreeing at once.
Hauling it into the square—the drinking, the feast,

the tangles of hungry limbs, & she & I in the grain.
Then the long moments of silence. Houses

in flames, the city disappearing. The blade I never felt
enter my chest—the smell of bread in her hair—

darkness. Darkness. Kissing the back of her knee.

Trevor Ketner

Gunshot Shards of Tiny, Steel Stars

I watched the clay pigeons whine toward the hill
    at the wide end of the dead
grass fan where I summoned the goddess Diana.
    Arms ivory in the sun, legs
warm buttermilk poured, perhaps what was left
    over after the ten biscuits
we made in the morning. I awoke in the country.

As their carrot clay flesh unfurled itself like frost
    in colors along the bank,
I imagined how I might shoot a pheasant midflight.
    How like a lapsed comet,
feather-tail trailing or the wild veering of blood
    vessels in shattered wings.
Clip the bird. Watch it spin into a 2nd amendment

constellation, into a nebula of yellow, yellow grass.
    All the little stars are shards
in a leaden astrology. I know how they get there,
    in a bursting, in a hurry,
through a grooved tunnel and out into all that light.

sam sax

gay boys and the bridges who love them

it is not the fall, exactly. not the crash either, the swallow,
      the life flashing backwards behind the dark screen of the eyes,
         the water rising up to meet you.

no. it is not what drove your body here like a stolen car.
      why you abandoned it on this unreasonable ledge. not why
         you dove in, salt wind singing its perfect punctuation.

it is not the city stretching out before you waving
      its startled steel hands. it is not the last man who turned
         you down, or turned you out, or turned the camera on.

it is not the six seconds between here and impact,
      though each is its own poem. it is not how the body
         overflows like a damned river into its ocean,

the shopping mall of chemicals doing their patient
      and awful sorting. not the suit of clothing you decided
         to die in, the wrinkled cotton jacket and its wet lineage.

the necktie and its perfect knot. it's not even the difference
      between being pushed and choosing to leave.

no. it is the wreckage
      spilling from the wreckage.

         it is the light
            throwing its last shade.

Ellene Glenn Moore

At Puget Sound I Think of My Brother

Did these mountains / too / grow

deep and fat from a pebble planted in the water / shadows

rising over the city / Another ocean

fills my mouth / Once

in a café / my brother called me / his voice so small

full of thorns always / even in daylight when we played in dune grass

riptide pulling / sand to sea

But it was dark on that call / and it was a darkness that unfolded from
    within him and I could only taste

its shadow / doubled through airwaves to where I sat / hot tea before me

steam rising like pain leaving the body

and it tasted like the bourbon he hid in the closet / preparing

for this night / for this phone call / waiting for me

to say that chrysanthemums are a bitter chew

that the lonely water pooling between our organs is the same

Here / across the Sound that is pricked

by caps of waves / some small trees reach upwards

What do mountains say / to their shadows

Michael Lavers

Patmos Revisited

No green clouds hang like a divine disease,
no hot breath haunts the back of the neck,
no claws clink their dictation across shale.
Oyster-shell sand still scatters the light, but songs
the sea here murmurs seem scum-fringed, colloquial,
its rhythms private and indifferent
to us; no tides of purple crabs rising
through town, bearing the dead back down to sea.
And dreams, when they happen now, are dreams:
we bore each other with them over breakfast.
No sun's blunt fist, no bruise of earth; instead,
leaf-colored leaves, and cow-faced cows,
and nameless toads that spook us while we sleep;
a perfect darkness making shadows disappear,
nights punctuated by someone downshore,
braining an octopus against a stone.

Kasey Erin Phifer-Byrne

The Real Birth of Venus

It wasn't out of a scalloped shell
like the birth
of any kind of pearl

It was exactly like all the others—
screaming and bearing down
spoonfuls of castor oil

My mother first pushed out
every other planet

and yes, there was a bit of foam
at the edge of her lips—
on the right side because the right

is the side of holiness
is the side of the hand of any god

But there were no gods there
because this was a mortal thing

this pain, her bones opening like mouths
to allow me passage
closing again to keep in my ghost

until the cord had frayed
and the lotus was dying

If there was anger in the universe
she felt it wholly

If there was love in the universe
she felt it wholly

If there was fear in the universe
she ate it whole

We knelt and prayed afterwards
and yes, it was to ourselves

David Thacker

A Fetus Dreams Her Father's Brain Is a Tenement

This is all such inadequate masonry,
   this blue ribboned with glass I tap, tap.
         I tire of tapping. My cerebrum casts shadows
  as long as yours now. You've called me up, a habit

         of rubbing your hairline, poor bronze
between thumb and middle finger. What can this genie tell
  except yourself? No Metis councils
      from your belly. And consider, in the story,

   while Metis murmurs up among the god's
  liver and spleen, another voice wrestles in her womb.
What conspiracy! But in you, no gravid mother
      banging out armor. Racket beyond loneliness:

  your longing. Is this the burnished metal
      you would wrap me in? This image of me
     you haunt yourself with? Which is
    really an image of you. You,

      still an Adam naming the creatures
  brought into view. An Eve wants all a body
    has to tell: the vocal shards humming
through the heart and the fetal leap—this suffering

like a god might suffer, this joy,
          random and planned
    as rain, as menstrual blood, as a child
become like one of us. A little pressure in a palm

      and the fruit's spines flex, dimple skin.
Opened, whatever its name, the flesh
           erupts on the tongue. Any Eve eats
               more than one.

Amy Woolard
A Place Where There Isn't Any Trouble

Girl walks into a house & comes out running. Girl runs down

A neighborhood street & a pickup rolls up beside her. Storm's

Coming. Aunt says Girl you know there're monsters out there

& you never know. Aunt says Sugar this storm'll run roughshod

Over the dirt you call childhood, farm & storm spread so wide they

Each get a name. Whiskey rolls down her throat & lights the farm

On fire. Aunt says Girl, there're monsters in this world you'll call

Friends in the next, storms that'll write your name in the sky,

Clouds that roll up & announce you like a choir. A fire don't

Chase but it catches. The bells of the neighborhood church keep

Pealing on without you & do not call you home. Around here,

Ugly ain't a name for the way somebody looks, but how she talks or

Talks back. *Rotten* isn't just for apples; it's for how she acts. Girl walks

Into the woods & comes out a monster. Storm kicks up beside her.

Mongrel paces just behind her footfall. There're farms in this world,

But Girl & Mongrel are headed to the next. Around here, strip

Where a field meets the woods is called *the Invitation*. Stray piece

Of straw on her skirt like an unlit match. Stray light splintering

Through the branches like tangled hair. Oh & she is lit

With whiskey now. Now a fugue settles over the trees.

Now a path undresses itself in front of her, fingers her

Forward. On the other side of an invitation, somebody's always

Cooking up something. Trouble is a dish. A prayer: *Fill my plate*

With sugared apples. Fill my heart with discipline. Mongrel cases

Any new body might stand in her way. If you can't beat them,

Join them, the farm calls. If you can't join them, let them

Walk you to your truck but when it's time to go, it's time to go,

The bells peal. Girl peels off her Sunday skirt like a bell gone

Soft. An invitation is just another line to be crossed, after all,

All of it rinsed with a light, salted. Girl leaves the farm lit

Behind her, but takes the path with her when she goes,

Wherever she goes, pretty as you please. Full of sugared

Breath to waste on the crook of the next one's neck. The dirt

I could dish, thinks Mongrel, *I'm the one she'll miss the most.*

Well, shoot. Somebody got to be the one who stands burning

On the porch, waves Aunt, & somebody got to be the one to get lost.

Eduardo Martinez-Leyva

Confirmation

That year we grew more and more
into our shared grief, hid in the ditch,
marred by snow-mold,

to drink bum wine,
then gossip about stars, mothers,
you-know-what. We rubbed beeswax

in our hair, watched our ends split.
On Sundays, we'd stare at the back
of the schoolteacher's glowing head.

Sweat halo, no bigger than a mare's
bite. After the lake thawed, and his body
surfaced, I heard his lips

were slightly open, as if in a calm,
permanent prayer. You heard this, too.

Cassie Donish
What Happened

Sometimes her voice gets low
like she's telling me a secret.

I think people can't listen
to certain kinds of stories,
she says. When they start

to hear it, they start
to change it, to listen instead
to their fear.

It changes memory.
That's why when I told
what happened,

it was misunderstood.
People heard
their own fear: the stranger

at the door. His bouquet
of pallid flowers.

Ian Burnette

Harvests

I

We used to play pirates
in an empty field

near my uncle's house,
the unshy earth

filling our hands
with oil beetles

and the odd penny
spoon—as if she

could resent us
for pulling thorns

from her shoulder.

II

Then there was the year
the ocean dried,

an oilman's angry
turbo diesel scraping

the barnacled road
that cleaved the farm

into calcium dust,
his pitch hair

and the cold metal pen
in my uncle's hand—

for the lease of the land,
he was promised

yellow gold, a hardy
flower called rapeseed

with canola in its veins.

III

By spring, bright bud
rucked our field

like a floodlight, a beam
the color of house clams

or razor flies. Stalks
ate past my uncle's

hungry waist and
sucked the land jaundice

with open mouths,
until three boys from town

took a quiet girl into
the belly of our field

and made her open up.

Antonina Palisano

For H

who called

I.

I still don't know   what to say
I dream I am a hawk
in a crested hood   I dream I feel
the handler's glove   its hated ballast   You ask
how a girl   digs out
I remember   the drop in pulse   A rush
that mimics flight   Heave   as if the earth
were complicit
Everything I've done   I have done   to myself
Chosen   the small concern   the sinew

II.

I think I told your father you would be fine which is statistically an
   unconscionable lie

III.

I ended   by dint of anger
It was another choice   to seek ground
To rage   at the dizzy breadth

which was not   breadth   but the false horizon
of an irregular heartbeat
the suggestion   of difference   Of real topography
A good jaunt   A world laid out

                                        In discovering
            I was pacing   stumbling   at that
            I recovered   mostly in spite   Irascible
            that I'd ever been   so neatly fooled

IV.

What I mean to give:
This is not flight
It's spurious
Tell me when you last felt
The actual motion of any part
Not the gullet
The heart in its somersault
Or the knuckles
Scored against the back teeth

V.

Although I also wake up every morning which is theoretically improbable
            given the circumstances

VI.

In another dream   I am unhooded
The broken wing   is a dull pain
Almost not a pain anymore

The glove   becomes a warmer thing   Human
in its warmth   Maybe there's no glove
Maybe I stand on a bare arm   I can't look
I'm mesmerized   by a cup of coffee

          Whole milk   one sugar   the good stuff
          strong   with real texture to it

Cristina Correa

Reflection from a Bridge

Look back and the park echoes
a bloom of unpicked strangers.
in the foreclosed shadows of trees.
under needling seeds
more than men who follow.
and see themselves comfortably
of teeth at empty-faced weddings,
birds' wings teardrop red,
the weeds, erasing
a geometry
The problem
is that

springtime. A woodpecker's hollow,
How they flourish and regenerate
How they burn and fade
of sunlight. This pastoral demands
Who visit this place to ruin the sod
aging. More than a backdrop
a rush of black-
frantic plastic bags choking
each other. Claiming
of survival.
with history
it becomes something else.

Stephanie Ellis Schlaifer

From the Cabinet of Counterweights & Measures

The raincloud floated swiftly by
      It floated   exuberantly
      lavishly, even   with admirable speed
      as though it were a barge
      (and urgently)
      with somewhere to go

And beneath its gouache-gray hull
you were   demonstrably marveling   at the living
patterns   of water   on water   on water

What is the weight of it worth to you?
      Its underbrushing
      Its sea of seas

             Is it captained? Navigable?

Can it steer the stations of your discord   wide and barren
as a moor?

For you are standing in a rising water—

the air is evident   the air, an exit   the air, untethered
barrage balloons

Why not reach upwards?   Rush headlong?
It is magnificent!

For here is nothing:
a drowsy, creatureless rain
where you are an idler   some tiny thing
frantically waving its hands

Analicia Sotelo

I'm Trying to Write a Poem About a Virgin and It's Awful

She was very unhappy and vaguely religious so I put her at the edge of the lake where the ducks were waddling along like Victorian children, living out their lives in blithe, downy softness. She hated her idleness. I loved her resilience. Her ability to turn her gaze on small versions of herself seemed important. The lake wasn't really a lake. It was a state of mind where words like *ochre, darken* and *false* were supposed to describe her at her best and worst, but they were only shadows and everyone knows the best shadows always look like the worst kinds of men. She wanted them badly, so I took her for a swim. In the lake that was not a lake, her twenty-five-year-old body felt the joy of being *bare* and *naïve* among the seaweed and tiny neon fish, but I didn't believe her. And I couldn't think of anything to say in her defense. Some people said I should take her out of the poem. Other people said *No*, take her out of the lake and put her in a bedroom where one man is saying, *I can't help you*, and another is saying, *You waited too long*. My ducks grew into lithe, cynical seabirds. When they said *Virgin* what they really meant was *Version we've left behind*. I didn't trust them. So I took her to the rush of the sea. She waded in and waved at me. I turned away. It wasn't her fault. She wasn't the shell I was after.

NOMINATED BY *The Antioch Review*

Elizabeth Metzger
Not Spring

When all the other trees are bare
the red tree grows.

The fire of a thousand parrots
cannot overcome its courage.

I picture you lying in the township
of your father's arms.

The noose of your mouth
is a way of not speaking.

The floors of your eyes, shiny
and light-soaked.

Rest finds your ribcage.
It hides and seeks within

the crescent lung,
a sad little Mesopotamia.

I will be talking to you
for a long time when you wake

in the felt shade, leaving
what you love of what you love.

NOMINATED BY COLUMBIA UNIVERSITY

Jaydn DeWald

Desire Lines

I place my hand in the small of your back—
A smooth, flesh-colored bowl
                              I once filled with water
  And drank from, in dusk-light, like a deer
In the quiet center of a forest—so that when you speak,
  When your response to my childish claim
That the world could be burning
                              and I'd still be happy—
  I see us, briefly, amid falling volcanic ash
And black leaves, naked, all set to repopulate the earth—
  Is, simply, half turning round to study me:
"But I love the world"—well, then,
                              my hand vibrates,
  Your voice in the quiet center of my hand
Vibrates and crescendoes and then courses through me
  Like a spirit singing through the long, red-
Carpeted halls of my body,
                              and all my vague idealism
  About us as two lovers, tucked in shadow
In a pool of ferns under a private moon in a lyric poem,
  Has if not disappeared—you're still there,
After all, trembling above me,
                              aqueous and moon-pale—
  Then at least deteriorated, photodegraded
By the late, eucalyptus-scented, summer morning light
  Of your skin, here, *right here*, at the head

Of our bed

   that now rises, behind curtained windows,
 In a quiet uncurtained corner of the world
Amid a field of flowers, human-faced, opening for you—
 The two of us, each with an inward flame
Burning on the red,

      rose-petal-strewn altar of the other,
 Made public now, together, made to exist
In full view beside or under or on top of or deep inside
 One another, dawn after wet purple dawn,
The sheets shushing like a faint shore under us—

         thus—

James Davis May

An Existential Bear

> "Nothing exists until it is observed."
> —*John Archibald Wheeler*

The theory is that to perceive something
is to create it, or rather to help to create it.
Until then, those mountains and the trees
drilling through their soil, and the afternoon moon
above them, occur, at best, as probabilities—
that the universe has created beings
to rescue it from that probability into existence.
So by turning to look at it, the old man
on top of another mountain makes Vermont
throw itself together in the July heat
the way individual cartoon bees assemble
into a swarm the moment they realize
the bear has reached into their hive.
The swarm becomes a fist, a pair of scissors,
finally an arrow before the bear concludes
that these are the wrong sort of bees.
Or consider the real bees in the first hours of spring
mobbing the early-blooming plum tree,
the bees my daughter fears, so we tell her
to stand still, like a statue, when they approach.
Only two years old, there's not a world
that she can imagine in which she is not seen,
so she flails at each buzz. By evening, though,

we've explained away the fear: she understands
that the bees don't want her, that they want flowers.
"So that they can turn them into honey,"
I tell her. "Yes," she says, "so I can eat it."

Erin L. Miller
Half-Life

Eventually you realize the self has nothing
to do with you. Your skin full of mirrors.
He held the back of your skull as if cupping
a spoon and you felt something lift out.
Every person you meet, more of you lifting out.
Your mornings spent finding parts,
putting them back in the way you want.
Your nights spent listening: all the species of you
howl at once. With what sharp pleasure
you would welcome stillness into your life.
Anyone would be tricked into thinking
this is a life—but there are other ways.
One day, a younger version of you will stand
at the door. She will hold a bowl of ripening fruit.

Jessica Nordell

Girl, Running

> "Whatever you make of this book, I need it."
> —*John Edgar Wideman*

Along the edge of the park
a girl is running barefoot
at the top of a ledge, the girl is four
or five, the ledge is six inches wide
she's moving fast, the trees are rising behind her
like dense green thunderheads
on each side of her pigeons
burble and brake, pedaling backward
in air she runs
past the screech of the occupied sandlot,
the voices split open, distorted in heat, she pulls
past the ice cream truck struck to a white metal blaze,
the screak and crawl of the street, the sun
is warming the limestone she runs on, the wind
is lapping the grit from her body,
and the flanks of the truck flicker heatless and dumb
as the televised blitz of a city.
The meters are flashing their blank
exhortations, the sun is pitched
like a snare, beating time.
Don't speak to her.
If she keeps her eyes on the stone
she can run this way
for a long time.

J.P. Grasser
Well

You took spent shotgun shells down
from the shelf, filled them to the lip
with blent black powder, hot-glued
fuses into their mouths to shut them up.
Even as a boy I knew their power.
Like clockwork, each time the well
clogged, you'd take one, spark it
with your cigarette, toss the screaming
charge into its closed throat. I imagined
the ribbed plastic casing bursting
at the middle in white-hot strobe.
What surprised me was the absence
of sound when one blew—just a plink
and a gentle plume—like a wished-on
penny. I think of you dying, your lungs
filled with fluid, a cruel inversion to life
on the fish farm. After the bypass,
they put you on nitrates. Your worn-out
jeans traded for gym shorts, boots
for Velcro no-slips. I didn't know
you. We fished together anyway, and once
I dragged up a largemouth, bigger than any
before. Your hand on mine, we eased
the blade into the metallic mesh of her ribcage.
Out burst more blackness than I believed.
I could only see fire lapping up the diesel-

slick iridescence—like the look of certain
change—as it spilled into my palms.
I know now it was shells, eggs ready
to explode with life. When you saw me shaking,
you said *roe*, though I could not imagine
to what far shore, or with what sturdy boat.

Cody Ernst
Come Up

I am biking up a hill toward a great-grandfather who hates me. The hill is
  the wettest,
      sun-soaked thing
I've ever ridden up, and buses of townspeople line the streets.
     They'll see me hated
by the great-grandfather. They'll see that hair dye has blackened his nails.
     Your ass is grass, he will say, your ass is pussy-willow weeds.

I am biking up a hill towards a Caribbean place where silk sheets billow in the trees.
     My mask is black and has straw whiskers.
Its mouth is the widest, reddest thing I've ever seen on my face.
     Toucans throw coconuts
onto hot-dog tourists cavorting in the shade.
     Farmers'-market stalls line the rim of an eggcup.

I'm biking up a hill towards a heavenly lamp. A circle of townspeople rides up
  around me.
     For now, I hum a song from a chain-gang movie.
I hum a part about beating rocks and swallowing sand.
     When we reach the lamp, I'll introduce myself to the townspeople.
When we're up there, crying in a pack around the lamp's glass,
     I'll shake their hands and say my name.

Danni Quintos
White Beauty

My sister & I watch a commercial:
Filipina beauties washing their faces.

Two sisters splash water like diamonds,
velvety suds. They are twins with black silk

hair & smooth, pink apple cheeks.
They are both whiter than any relatives

we've met here, whiter than the quiet Welsh
& Japanese blood in both of us. On the screen

a blind date in a blazer rings the doorbell.
The more porcelain sister answers—

her fluorescence lights his stupid smile.
The door opens wider to reveal her

healthy-glow twin: apricot flushed
next to the sharp, pallid sister. The man frowns.

We frown, knowing that the next scene
will be the sister sharing her secret

potion: just use Pond's White Beauty
to bleach the sun from your skin,

to make you milky transparent:
white, snow, chalk, paper.

The second date he sees them both
glowing ghostly identical, laughing

at how beautiful they've both become,
unable to tell which girl is his date.

We are two sisters in this middle of the world
heat, sweating to the hum of fans. In the dark

instant between commercials, our brown faces
appear in the TV's glass.

Allison Adair
Western Slope

The women who come here partly give up
being women. No last names, no locks.
A spike, instead, concealed in every hairbrush.
A man's a bear, a cub embeds his claw
in the hollow door. You wear it on a string.

Your own first snow melts gradually, old firn
riding the continental divide back to a distant
ocean. We swam there once, that water, alien blue
algae pulsing like a showgirl in the wings, it was
when you shot the worn dog that I knew you

had gone for good. Even cakes struggle to rise
at 10,000 ft. Hard angles to the atmosphere, you
say. A newborn fits a thick palm. Blood stretches
too, gasping, for its sliver of air. You won't come
down, everything now's an open mouth to the wide sky and the sky unspooling
cloudless and cloudless and cloudless.

(But—before I go—wasn't it us for a while? Weren't we the neon
kicking in the light? Tell me you remember the waves
bathing our necks, our small ears?)

Claire Wahmanholm

Fallow

Follow the field into its summer, into its faun-colored heat,
its tall, feathery yarrow.
　　　　　　　Look down at the untilled clouds breathing
in the pond, whose water is so shallow and shadowless it's hot.
Harrows withdraw to the horizon, dragging wide, weeded furrows
for you to lay your body in.
　　　　　　　What a bad year it's been. What a slow
wallow of a season.
　　　　　　Lay it down. Lay it down and wait
for the cross plough's hatch and scatter. Remember the fish pond
and its clouds, its stalks of swamp rose mallow, the wide-leafed sallows.
Remember the hollow smell of waiting.
　　　　　　　Soon, haying. But not until
your teeth are tilled, are tilth. Not until the rhizomes of your bones
have been pulled and killed.
　　　　　　Lie low and let the swallows pick you clean.
When the future comes it will rise green as a willow from your yellow eyes.

NOMINATED BY THE UNIVERSITY OF UTAH

Crystal C. Karlberg
Bees Make Me Think of My Mother

They need to be anesthetized
to give up their sweetness, but
willingly surrender pleasure
for more or better pleasure.
There is always better pleasure
somewhere, with some other
flower, some other daughter.
I like to imagine her on her knees
in the dirt. If that makes me
a bad person, then so be it.

When the neighbor's son
finally found his calling,
she took me to see the buzzing
boxes stacked on buzzing boxes.
I wanted some honey, anything
to soothe the sinking feeling,
not hunger, but knowledge,
bees know, but children don't.
I was not like most children.

When I drank from the beehive bottle,
it was like diving into the blue
of her robe again and again,
the cigarette butts fell away

and everything was snap-
dragons and zinnias, strawberries
growing in between the stones,
the humming of the drones
as they tried to please their queen.

Clare Paniccia
I Wish I Could Say

that I did not throw mud at Peter—I wish
I could say that I had been good, and not privy
to boys and their spit, their curled hair

and ripped uniforms, always huddling together
behind the youth house and pissing sideways
onto the brick. I wish I could say that I didn't

lift my skirt under the lunch table, Brian
eyeing the smooth crevice and slipping me
a quarter—Later, that night, I might have tried

to shave nothing, and bled. I wish I had avoided
the gravel lot, the forest of weeds circling
around rusted fence, the boys daring us

to squat and pee onto church bulletins—And didn't
everyone else run away but me, crouched down,
convincing myself that this would make some

difference in the way they all would watch;
the piss wandering down my leg and soaking
into sock, the aide dragging me into

the gymnasium. I wish I hadn't been
embarrassed by that blossoming womanhood,
envying cock and all the things boys might get

away with: their clubs and their hatred, and me.
I wish I could say I nested my shame like a
matryoshka doll, those separate faces wrapping

into each other, sequestering hot panic—
Instead, it fought to bubble forth:
my fingers seeking weapons from

the Earth and flinging whatever I could pull out
toward those bodies that mocked me.

NOMINATED BY SOUTHEAST MISSOURI STATE UNIVERSITY

Marci Calabretta Cancio-Bello

Songs of Thirst: Six Sijo

Here, the deer, having no tusks, grow great bone branches from their skulls.
Here, they cannot wound the water, and their thirst is so small,
even in the rutting season. Not like ours. Not like mine.

*

Once, when I was eleven, I saw the fish-oil hand cream
scented with crushed jasmine petals, how Grandmother's fingers daubed
then smoothed over the hard backs of her hands. Only once I saw this.

*

Grandmother's fingers binding a dragonfly body with silk,
unspooling the thread, knotting it around my thumb for a kite.
Her hand hard against my face for letting it slip so soon.

*

There are many kinds of thirst: that of the sea for the shore,
potted roots for the forest floor, woman for a man she does not have—
father, lover, son—that which thickens and blackens the tongue.

*

How many times we counted the stars in our constellations—
the rooster, the tiger, the boar, and mine, which should have been the horse.
All this to keep from counting the sons who drowned when no one was near.

*

Daily I swallow the bitter branch of my brother's absence.
No water still is sweet enough to slake this ghostly thirst.
But this is not a love song, nor a glossary of despair.

Jessica Bixel
Lullaby for a Changeling

I've made the boy a mule deer.
He has ruined his mouth with the winter grass.

He has chased into red leaves,
into the ready seam of sleep. Too, he has sorrow.

He says dear sun with a tongue made salt.
Says, *it still feels like something undone.*

Here there are no dreams but in fables.
I didn't write this story.

Where his legs turn to fallow there is a dawn pretending.
Wrecked belly. Trembling. *Says, I can't agree with you.*

Ask me if I made him wild. Ask me, what is losing
to the forest? What is beginning again?

Laura Bylenok
Infinite Regress

The world is flat.
The world is flat and it sits on a kettle.
I mean a turtle.
No, I mean a tortoise.
I mean, I can walk all the way home from here
with a hot toddy in my pocket
and not get wet. Can't I? Oh, I can
all the way before the kettle whistles
before here I am in the backseat with the law
and it was a siren after all.
They told me Jupiter has sixty-seven wives
and he raped them all.
When we fly by the cornfield
I'll point out that one weird white cow
grieving like a moon
but they won't understand.
The doors were locked.
I never meant to come along
and the night's still heaving at a crawl.
Shit the world is flat out here.
We can see it all, as if
there was no such thing as terrified.
It was like I told the law,
just please just let me out.
I was just leaving.
I'm telling you this because you know

it's true: all my little lies are infinite.
They held me down
and I lowed as long and loud as a planet.

NOMINATED BY *PLEIADES*

Brian Leary
Wolf for Water

At the Brooklyn promenade, above Lady Liberty's harbor,
the dogs come undone: their tongues

slung out like balls on rope, faces skipping seaward, landward.

Even without knowing why they love this place so goofily,
I like that they do. Because evening

can be such a letdown. My bones a stringless heap

in the day's comedown, but how to mend them.
I had meant to be grand, not some fox going gray.

Some wolf for water. Mustering for upswing. The tide below swallowing

those closest, furthest. The ocean, I think,
the ocean gets it—this stone-dumb want—this American

thing—to wash & wash anew: as if water

makes anything of the beach but beach already there.
But those silly dogs—they, too, are on & on

with the same string: they just love love, love love.

Ashley Keyser
Land of Flowers

1.

All the dads they have ever met
haunt their wardrobes, these scrubbed young men,
five abreast on the sidewalk. Five pastel polos,
each a different shade, like candy buttons,
or like the brassy condos flaunting their newness
on Clearwater Beach, where the sand irked you
("too disorganized") but you took off your shirt,
even though you didn't want to be seen.
As the orange-tinted boys' boat shoes
slap vigorously toward us, we give way
to let their handsome health pass by.
We linger, like old news, in the gutter.

2.

"It's not that I'm shallow. It's just
his lazy eye is *so* distracting." The girls
in the next booth can't stop agreeing,
their bowl-sized glasses tinkling. "Honey,
I know. You're *so* not shallow." Drinks here
have names like Blowjob and Fuzzy Dick,
so we order ours neat. You're purple
in harsh light, like a Toulouse-Lautrec painting
sunk in bathwater. "The real lazy thing,
if you ask me, is he doesn't fix that eye.
All this modern medicine." A few blocks down,

the tide writhes at the earth's feet, a sound
drowned out by the game on plasma screens.

3.
August, when we "take a break," flakes off
in piles of termite wings, what the fuckers shed
before banqueting on my house. Florida,
like its cockroaches, eats everything, yawning
sinkhole-mouths—under some guy's bed,
even, while he slept! I sleep alone,
your salt and aftershave scenting the pillow.
Vines thread the shingles, as if no one
ever lived here. When I open *Anna Karenina*,
two termites breed in the cover, wriggling
and flightless, a smudged ex libris.

4.
The vasectomy surgeon's missing-link brow
jabs at us from its billboard (1-800-VAS-TIME)
as you in the driver's seat grab my wrist
and stuff my whole hand into your mouth.
I'd like to buy you something you don't need:
fifteen boxes of berries from a roadside stand,
or the gas station's basket of toy kittens
plastered in unnervingly realistic fur.
In answer to another billboard's challenge,
"If you die tonight—HEAVEN or HELL?!"
you call the hotline: "I hope you aren't bored
or lonely." All the way home, I can't stop
touching the silky down on your nape.

Edgar Kunz

My Father at 49, Working the Night Shift at B&R Diesel

There's no one left to see his hands
      lifting from the engine bay, dark and gnarled
           as roots dripping river mud.

No one to see how his palms—slabs of callus
      from scouring the long throats of chimneys,
           hauling mortar and brick—move

in the fabricated light. The thumb-knuckle
      thick and white as a grub where the boxcutter
           bit. The split nail grown back

scalloped and crooked. The stitch-puckered
      skin. And when they fold into and out
           of themselves by the steaming faucet,

when they strip clean, the tapwater
      running black, then copper, then clear
           into the grease-clotted drain,

there's no one to witness the slap
      of a wet rag tossed in the breakroom
           sink or the champ of gravel

in the empty lot. How the stars dim
      as morning comes on. How a semi downshifts
           on the overpass and the shop-

windows rattle as it goes.
    How my father drags his body into a beat-up van
        and gropes for the ignition.

Damian Caudill

Tuesday Ordinary

"I think the hoodie is as much responsible for Trayvon Martin's death as George
Zimmerman was."
—*Geraldo Rivera speaking on* Fox and Friends, *March 23, 2012*

T, the storm clouds are glaring blue today,
but we walk the blocks to the gas station anyway.
      The stone-polishing sweat of you in my pocket.
          My throwback cotton blend,
              my name-fuckin'-brandness.

When you put me on I hang loose from your body
because even in February this is still boiling Florida
and we have survived our whole lives here, ground
into parking lots like asphalt and beach sand
from better places.

You know I hate the closet and the bedroom floor.
Hate that there are months when you do not pull
me on over ratty t-shirts or the kick of new cologne.

No doubt, the snow won't show up again this year.
How much I want to lock in the stick-thin heat of you,
to keep out whatever bad day is always following us home.

And I do love the fat sidewalks in Sanford.
Love that we tour them alone during weekdays
built like intermissions, the whole town
slouched down in their seats, every neighbor
calling out for backup as we pass.

Christopher Kempf

Disaster Capital; or, We Are Made of Stardust & Will Explode

is the kind of thing I said then, desperate
for any woman I knew to let me
be, for her, that doomed beauty I believed
in still. That was the summer construction
stopped. Beyond the city the scaffolded
frames of half-finished mansions rose, bone-like
& empty against the night while, inside
an abandoned Colonial open,
as yet, to the sky above it, I watched
with Leah Mackenzie the wheeling web
of light beginning to turn. Technically,
it is true. Inside the Big Bang the same
square-millimeter of carbon became
both Pleiades & each small breast she let
fall to me in our dark bower. & we
were young in those days, yes, & staring up
we seemed at the bright center of some high
spectacular devastation claiming
everything. Stocks fell. Wars were on. Across
the suburbs the streets' scrollwork, zoned, we knew
for water & light, lay empty. Playgrounds
waited for their children. In fields, fire
hydrants blossomed. I wanted, romantic
that I was, that full stop astronomers
predict will happen someday. Disaster,
dictionaries say, meant misalignment
of the stars once I wanted that. Rather,

morning came. Colors returned. Together
we dressed. *Desuetude*, Proust calls it, an object's
or person's long pedestrian descent
into ruin. Wiring stripped, the streetlights
of Foxglove Glen led us back. Above us,
the sunrise—rosy, we call it—clotted.

Elizabeth Onusko

Former Future King

The world you grew up in is no longer
yours. The ruins of the palace are gilded
with dandelions, and you live in an apartment
above the shop where you work as a mechanic.
Most weekends, you take a bus to the art museum
and sit on a bench in front of the crown
you ought to have worn, which resides on a pillow,
in a locked glass box, in the furthest wing.
You long ago memorized the solid gold curves,
the auroras dilating from gemstones
and blending into a corona,
the soft, feathered quality of which
reminds you of the sunset
the day your father was assassinated
and you hid alone in a forest, watching the sky
flush yellow-orange as if being forged,
when suddenly the trees shrank down to saplings,
then disappeared underground. You started blinking
erratically, uncontrollably; your lids sealed shut
and your eyes rewound all they had seen
in a rapid succession of dilations and contractions.
Every feeling you ever had came alive again
for a brief, bursting moment
until you arrived at the hour of your birth,
swaddled in a silk blanket and bestowed with
the promise that you were worthy

of worship. You linger awhile in the warmth.
Eventually, your mind returns you
to the bench upon which you are sitting,
to the box holding your crown,
to the emergency exit in the corner
illuminated with pin lights
that you will never open.

J.G. McClure

Ars Poetica

The jazz hall was built 40 feet underground
to keep concerts in and streetsounds out—

a wonderful idea and an incredible
fire hazard. So the city shut it down and now

it's stuffed with boxes, barrels, and scrapped pianos.
This is the perfect place for the pianos.

Think of the rats. At night (it's always night)
they must scamper across keys

that sometimes work,
playing scales no one hears

but that scare the rats shitless,
driving them faster and faster along the shifting ivory floor

clanging and banging, filling
the moss-damp hall with a music

they want nothing at all to do with,
and when it's over they sniff the dark

for whatever it was that chased them
because it must be out there still

and if only they could smell it at least
they'd know which way to run.

Alicia Rebecca Myers

The Last Travel Agent

She hides honey in a globe.
Her hair smells of camphor.
Mornings, children scatter
heirlooms. Their fingers work the ash.
Here is a mesh of lace. Here is a rope
of felt. Sometimes the stones become the fragile
cups and saucers she once laid out for friends.
Remember the sky
strewn with paper lanterns?
The moon as anything other
than dread? O bird with one wing
heavier than the other.

Air splinters. Like a Medusa head
the capstan glowers.
Geography is spent.
Line them up, line them up.
How does the fable go again? Enough stones
in the pitcher and the crow can drink.

Tiana Clark

The Frequency of Goodnight
after Terrence Hayes

> "The duende is not in the throat:
> the duende surges up, inside,
> from the soles of the feet."
> —*Federico García Lorca*

Like so many nights of my childhood
  I lived inside the fishbowl
of a one-bedroom apartment,
  waited for my mother to come home
(from her second job). As a waitress
  she wore orthopedic shoes for flat feet.
All the uniforms blur together: IHOP,
  Red Lobster, Rainforest Café, Shoney's…
This is how she tucked me in—
  jingle and clack of keys
would turn the doorknob open
  allow me to fall asleep.
She tucked me in—not with blankets
  or a kiss on the forehead,
but with locking the door behind her.
  My single mother would take those big,
boxy shoes off, unhook her bra
  (too tired to take it all the way off)
and eat the leftover pizza
  I had ordered for dinner.
Television shadows flickered

her exhausted frame, smell
of other people's food on her skin,
  crumpled ones, fives and tens
fanned out of her server book.
  I heard the change from bad tippers
like hail on the kitchen counter.
  Maybe for other children
the purr of the air conditioner, the sound
  of a ceiling fan whisking the darkness,
or the steady neon glow of a nightlight
  set their dreams ablaze?
But for me hearing those keys
  slipped me under the wing
of my mother's white noise.

Let me begin again,
  when I was a waitress during college,
I had the shoes that doctors and nurses
  wore to support their posture.
On Saturdays I worked doubles,
  toward the end of my two shifts
my pace would slow—
  as I made laps around my tables,
picked up half-eaten sandwiches,
  grabbed napkins with chewed gristle.
  When we closed,
I'd be on my hands and knees,
  as I swept up litter from the day,
collected broken-off ends of French fries,
  dislodged pucks of used gum,

dragged swollen and leaky trash bags
   to the dumpster.
Bone heavy and body tired—
   I would come home,
take those heavy wooden clogs off.
   Turn on some show and listen
to the cadence of dialogue
   like a metronome tipping my head
to the baptism of sleep.

Let me begin again,
   The first dead body I ever saw
was my grandmother. It was Alzheimer's—
   My mother said, *She always left*
that old TV on while she slept…
   frequencies messed with her head.
If I focus now, I can still see my mom
   asleep in her uniform on the couch—
feet propped up, open pizza box
   dappled in grease stains.
I would tiptoe and turn off the television
   slink back to our bedroom.
This is how I tucked her in.
   This is how we said goodnight.

Mary Angelino

Dinner at Nonna's

Her sons won't translate at the table
so my Nonna says *I love you,* has to use it

for everything—a heaping bowl of ragù,
a smudged glass of wine & Sprite on ice.

She'll use it to request her favorite
satin scarf, her eggplant lipstick kissed down

to its nub. She'll use it to show me
what's still good, what's gone bad,

how to shoo flies with a hiss & twitch,
our fingers purple from digging

to the armored hearts of artichokes
she'll soften in oil. & always,

she'll use it to keep me longer
when I have to go, to give me things

she thinks I'll use—this time, her shoes
decades old without a scuff or crease, except

the rubber on the heel-tips is gone, the tiny nails
exposed & worn down. My father mutters

something about repair as we wave from the car
& *I love you* is *Thank you* & *Goodbye.*

Michael Derrick Hudson
The Garden of Eden and the Trilobite

Eve sits back on her splendid haunches in a prospect
of daffodils, violets and cornflowers

with sun-dappled butterflies and birds of paradise

and a jet-black panther that'd never been anything
but purrs of feline solicitude, watching

to see if Adam decides to take a bite. *A starfish!*

he cries. *I was once a starfish! Then a trilobite
then an ichthyosaur then a pocket gopher*

then a red ruffed lemur! He hands it back and Eve

gnaws it down to the core. *What's with the bikini?*
he asks, puckering his brow. *How like*

a monkey, thinks Eve, a little unkindly. *O believe
me, this is how they'll want things*

from now on, she explains, letting a single rivulet
of sticky crimson nectar trickle down

the world's first décolletage. Spiders emerge and
the panther for the first time growls

and slinks away. In heaven someone or something
keeps blatting away on a warlike trumpet

while Adam attempts to sneak another look.

Emily Skaja
Four Hawks

circle the same mile of Indiana where I force myself to look

at every dead deer on the road, as if that braces me, as if I believe
it will protect me from losing anything good.

I can't stop dreaming I'm hiding

my own prints in the snow, convinced
my mouth is a metal trap, a part of it, apart

from you, & when you pull me awake
it's because I'm lining my body with burrs,

because I'm antlers & talons & I know

the smell of cedar is home, is a ring of sky
I love, but I can't take it when

you say *Only deer, only hawks.*

Why is there nothing wild in you
to explain it, nothing killing; why

am I the chased thing horrified
to overtake myself in the brush I wonder &

if a deer darts across this road & the dead don't
take it, don't the dead wait, don't I know,

don't the dead always covet something running?

I count bodies like cold days in March.

Ten, eleven, twelve—& you
with the map unfolded, following the sky.

I wonder if you & I are twin limbs
of something running.

If you & I circle.

Contributors' Notes

ALLISON ADAIR's poems have appeared or are forthcoming in *Boston Review*, *Mid-American Review*, *The Missouri Review* (Poem of the Week), *Tinderbox Poetry Journal*, *Tahoma Literary Review*, *The Journal of Compressed Creative Arts*, *The Boston Globe*, and the anthology *Hacks*; hypertext projects appear on *The Rumpus* and *Electric Literature*. Winner of the 2015 Orlando Prize and the 2014 Fineline Competition, Adair teaches at Boston College and Grub Street.

MARY ANGELINO's publications include *Best New Poets 2010*, *Nimrod*, *Shenandoah*, and *The Journal*; work is forthcoming in *New Ohio Review*, *Water-Stone Review*, and *Ninth Letter*. She is an Arkansas Arts Council fellow, and she edited for *Linebreak* in its early years. Originally from Los Angeles, she now lives in Fayetteville (where she earned her MFA) and teaches English at Northwest Arkansas Community College.

JESSICA BIXEL earned her MFA from Bowling Green State University.

IAN BURNETTE is a student at Kenyon College and an associate at *The Kenyon Review*. His work has appeared in *The Forward Book of Poetry*, *The Kenyon Review*, *The Adroit Journal*, *The 826 Quarterly*, and elsewhere. He lives in central Ohio.

LAURA BYLENOK's debut collection of poetry, *Warp*, was selected for the 2015 T.S. Eliot Prize and is forthcoming from Truman State University Press. She is also the author of the hybrid prose chapbook, *a/0* (*DIAGRAM* and New Michigan Press, 2014), and her poetry has appeared in journals such as *Pleiades*, *North American Review*, *West Branch*, and *Guernic*a, among others. She lives in Salt Lake City.

MARCI CALABRETTA CANCIO-BELLO has received poetry fellowships from Kundiman and the Knight Foundation. Her manuscript, *Hour of the Ox*, won the 2015 AWP Donald Hall Prize for Poetry. She serves as co-founding editor of *Print-Oriented Bastards*, a contributing editor for *Florida Book Review*, and producer of The Working Poet Radio Show. Visit her at marcicalabretta.com.

DAMIAN CAUDILL is a recent south Florida transplant from the foothills of Ohio. Currently he writes in the MFA program at the University of Miami where he is a James A. Michener fellow and was awarded the Academy of American Poets Prize in 2014. Recently, his poems have appeared in *Rattle*, *Ninth Letter*, and *Pleiades*. A selection of his creative and critical work is forthcoming next year in the anthology *It Was Written: Poetry Inspired by Hip-Hop*.

LEILA CHATTI is a Tunisian-American poet. She received her MFA from North Carolina State University. A recipient of an Academy of American Poets Prize and second place winner of The Pablo Neruda Prize for Poetry, her work appears or is forthcoming in *Rattle*, *Crab Orchard Review*, *Cimarron Review*, *Nimrod*, *Linebreak*, and others. She currently serves on the poetry staff at *The Adroit Journal*.

TIANA CLARK is a Pushcart Prize nominee and recent recipient of the 2015 *Rattle* Poetry Prize. She is an MFA candidate at Vanderbilt University and serves on the board for the nonprofit literary center The Porch Writers' Collective. Her work has appeared or is forthcoming in *The Raven Chronicles*, *Nashville Arts Magazine*, *Word Riot*, *Native Magazine*, *Rattle*, *Crab Orchard Review*, *The Adroit Journal*, and elsewhere. Visit her at tianaclark.com.

CRISTINA CORREA is a VONA/Voices writer and a Midwestern Voices and Visions awardee who has received fellowships from the Indiana University Writers' Conference and the Ragdale Foundation. Her poems have been published or are forthcoming in *TriQuarterly*, *MAKE: A Literary Magazine*, and *Vinyl Poetry*; broadcast on National Public Radio's *Latino USA*; and exhibited at the Museum of Contemporary Art Detroit. She holds a BA in creative writing from Columbia College and an MA in Latin American and Latino studies from the University of Illinois at Chicago.

J. JEROME CRUZ lives and writes in Homer Glen, Illinois. His poems have appeared in *Hayden's Ferry Review*, *New Delta Review*, *Cimarron Review*, *The Adroit Journal*, *RHINO*, and *Booth*.

JAYDN DEWALD is a writer, musician, and teacher. Recent work has appeared in or is forthcoming from *Beloit Poetry Journal*, *Columbia Poetry Review*, *december*, *Fairy Tale Review*, *Fourteen Hills*, and many others. He currently lives with his wife and daughter in Athens, Georgia, where he is a doctoral candidate in creative writing at the University of Georgia.

CASSIE DONISH's poems have appeared or are forthcoming in *Quarterly West*; *Sixth Finch*; *Jellyfish*; *Forklift, Ohio*; and elsewhere. An editor of *February, an anthology* and the literary magazine *The Spectacle*, she is currently an MFA candidate and Olin Fellow at Washington University in St. Louis. She holds an MA in cultural geography from the University of Oregon and hails from South Pasadena, California.

LISA DORDAL (MDiv, MFA), author of *Commemoration* from Finishing Line Press, teaches in the English Department at Vanderbilt University. Her poetry has appeared in a variety of journals including *CALYX, Cave Wall, Sojourners, New Millennium Writings,* and the *Journal of Feminist Studies in Religion.*

CODY ERNST is an instructor at The Writing Seminars at Johns Hopkins University. His work is appearing in *Drunken Boat; The Minnesota Review; Forklift, Ohio;* and elsewhere. He serves as a poetry editor of *The Adroit Journal.*

J.P. GRASSER's poetry explores the diverse regions he has called home, most insistently his family's fish hatchery in Brady, Nebraska. He studied English and creative writing at Sewanee: The University of the South and received his MFA in poetry from Johns Hopkins University. His work appears or is forthcoming from *32 Poems, Prairie Schooner, Crab Orchard Review,* and *West Branch Wired,* among others. He is currently a PhD candidate in poetry at the University of Utah, where he also teaches. Visit jpgrasser.com.

ALYSIA NICOLE HARRIS is a black woman Xian and hails from Alexandria, Virginia. She received her MFA in poetry from NYU and is currently a PhD candidate in linguistics at Yale University. A Pushcart nominee and winner of the 2014 and 2015 Stephen Dunn Poetry Prizes, her poetry has been published in *Indiana Review; Catch & Release, Columbia: A Journal of Literature and Art; Solstice Literary Magazine* and *Vinyl Magazine,* among others. As a performance artist, Alysia has toured nationally and has also performed in Canada, South Africa, Germany, Slovakia, and the UK. She is the 2015 Duncanson artist-in-residence at the Taft Museum of Art in Cincinnati and currently lives in New Haven, Connecticut.

MICHAEL DERRICK HUDSON lives in Fort Wayne, Indiana, where he works for the Allen County Public Library. His poems have appeared in *POETRY*, *Boulevard*, *Georgia Review*, *Gulf Coast*, *River Styx*, *New Ohio Review*, and other journals. He was co-winner of the 2014 Manchester Poetry Prize founded by Poet Laureate Carol Ann Duffy.

CRYSTAL C. KARLBERG is a graduate of the Creative Writing Program at Boston University. She read with Tupelo Press at the Mass Poetry Festival in May 2015. Her poems have been published in *Oddball Magazine*, *The Prompt*, *MadHat Lit*, and *Tupelo Quarterly*.

CHRISTOPHER KEMPF is the author of *Late in the Empire of Men*, which won the Levis Prize from Four Way Books and is forthcoming in March 2017. A recipient of a 2015 National Endowment for the Arts Fellowship and a Wallace Stegner Fellowship from Stanford University, his work has appeared in *The Gettysburg Review*, *Gulf Coast*, *Kenyon Review Online*, and *The New Republic*, among other places. He received his MFA from Cornell University, and currently lives in Chicago, where he is a PhD student in English literature at the University of Chicago.

TREVOR KETNER is an MFA candidate in poetry at the University of Minnesota. His work has appeared or is forthcoming in *The Adroit Journal*, *The Offing*, *The Rumpus*, *Cream City Review*, *The Journal*, *Bayou Magazine*, *Thrush Poetry Journal; Hayden's Ferry Review* and elsewhere. Recently he received the 2014 Gesell Award in Poetry and was a finalist for the 2014 *MARY* Editors' Prize and the 2013 Wabash Prize for Poetry. He serves as a poetry reader for *Slice Magazine*, and is the marketing assistant for Graywolf Press.

ASHLEY KEYSER is an MFA candidate at University of Florida. Her work has been published in *Nashville Review* and *Passages North* and is forthcoming in *Pleiades, The Cincinnati Review,* and *The Journal.*

EDGAR KUNZ is a Wallace Stegner Fellow at Stanford University. His work can be found in *New England Review, The Missouri Review, AGNI, Narrative Magazine,* and other places. His writing has been supported by the Bread Loaf Writers' Conference, the Academy of American Poets, and Vanderbilt University, where he earned his MFA. He lives in Oakland, California.

MICHAEL LAVERS's poems have recently appeared in *Smartish Pace, Arts & Letters, West Branch, 32 Poems, The Hudson Review,* and elsewhere. He teaches poetry at Brigham Young University.

BRIAN LEARY is a writer, attorney, rock climber, and vegetarian. His work has previously appeared in *Hayden's Ferry Review, The Gay & Lesbian Review, American Short Fiction, december,* and *The New York University Law Review,* among others. He lives in Brooklyn.

EDUARDO MARTINEZ-LEYVA's poems have appeared in *Assaracus, Apogee Journal, Nepantla: A Journal for Queer Poets of Color,* and elsewhere. He received his MFA from Columbia University, where he was a teaching fellow. He grew up in El Paso, Texas, and currently lives in New York City. He is a CantoMundo Fellow.

Originally from Pittsburgh, JAMES DAVIS MAY now lives in the Georgia mountains. His poems have appeared in *Ecotone, The Missouri Review, New England Review, The New Republic, The Southern Review,* and elsewhere. His first book of poems, *Unquiet Things,* will be published by Louisiana State University Press in 2016.

JOHN MCCARTHY is the author of the forthcoming collection *Ghost County* (MG Press, 2016). His poetry has appeared in *Redivider, The Minnesota Review, The Pinch, RHINO, Salamander,* and *The Jabberwock Review.* He is the managing editor of *Quiddity International Literary Journal and Public-Radio Program* and an MFA candidate at Southern Illinois University Carbondale.

J.G. MCCLURE holds an MFA from the University of California, Irvine. His poems and prose appear in *Gettysburg Review, Green Mountains Review, Nashville Review, The Pinch, Colorado Review,* and *Rain Taxi,* among others. He is the craft essay editor and assistant poetry editor of *Cleaver,* and is at work on his first collection. See more at jgmcclure.weebly.com.

ELIZABETH METZGER holds an MFA from Columbia University, where she was a University Writing teaching fellow. In 2013, she won the *Narrative* Poetry Contest. Her poems have most recently appeared in *The New Yorker, The Yale Review,* and *Kenyon Review Online,* and her essays have appeared in *Boston Review, Southwest Review,* and *PN Review.* She is the poetry editor of the *Los Angeles Review of Books Quarterly Journal.* Read more at elizabethmetzger.com.

ERIN L. MILLER earned her MFA in poetry at Bowling Green State University. Her poetry and reviews have appeared in *Bluestem, The Rumpus, Black Warrior Review, Linebreak,* and others. She was a finalist for *Sonora Review*'s 2015 Poetry Prize and the recipient of a Devine Fellowship in 2013.

ELLENE GLENN MOORE is an MFA candidate at Florida International University, where she holds a John S. and James L. Knight Foundation Fellowship in Poetry. Her work has appeared or is forthcoming in *Salamander, Bayou Magazine, Ninth Letter Online, Caliban,* and elsewhere. Find her at elleneglennmoore.com.

Lena Moses-Schmitt's work has appeared in *The Normal School, Devil's Lake, The Pinch, The Paris-American,* and elsewhere. She received her MFA in poetry from Virginia Commonwealth University, where she was the lead associate editor of *Blackbird.* She lives in Austin, Texas.

Alicia Rebecca Myers is a poet and essayist whose work has appeared most recently in or is forthcoming from *The Rumpus, Brain Child Magazine, The American Literary Review, Gulf Coast, jubilat, The Carolina Quarterly,* and *The Fairy Tale Review.* In February of 2014, she was awarded a residency at the Kimmel Harding Nelson Center in Nebraska City. A graduate of NYU's MFA Program, her chapbook *My Seaborgium* was selected for publication by Brain Mill Press for their 2015 Mineral Point Chapbook Series. She was a travel agent for seven years. You can find her online at aliciarebeccamyers.com

Jessica Nordell grew up in Green Bay, Wisconsin. She received her MFA from the University of Wisconsin-Madison, where she was the Renk Distinguished Graduate Fellow in Poetry. Her poetry and nonfiction have appeared in *The New York Times, FIELD, Slate, Salon,* and *The New Republic.* She lives in Minneapolis and works for the innovation consultancy Zeus Jones. About "Girl, Running," she writes, "When visiting my sister Lindsay in Brooklyn one summer, I was sitting outside Prospect Park and saw this little girl racing along the fence. Her energy shot her farther than I could see and propelled this poem."

Elizabeth Onusko's poems have appeared or are forthcoming in *Witness, The Journal, Slice Magazine, Linebreak, Southern Humanities Review, The Adroit Journal,* and *Vinyl Poetry,* among others. Her work has also been nominated for a Pushcart Prize and featured on *Verse Daily.* A founding editor of *Guernica,* she holds an MFA in poetry from Sarah Lawrence College and an MA in English with a writing concentration from Fordham University. Visit her at elizabethonusko.com.

ANTONINA PALISANO holds an MFA from Boston University, where she was awarded the 2015 Academy of American Poets Prize. Her work has appeared in *The Massachusetts Review, Washington Square Review, Potluck Magazine, Bellevue Literary Review,* and other publications, including the "World To Come" anthology produced for the *Jewish Currents'* Raynes Poetry Prize. She has taught creative writing at the high school and college levels and lives in Medford, Massachusetts.

CLARE PANICCIA was raised in upstate New York. Her poems have appeared in or are forthcoming from *The Cumberland River Review, The Pine Hills Review, The Cape Rock, Cave Region Review,* and elsewhere. She was a finalist for *Ruminate Magazine's* 2015 Janet McCabe Poetry Prize. Having received an MA in professional writing from Southeast Missouri State University, she is now pursuing a PhD in poetry at Oklahoma State University.

KASEY ERIN PHIFER-BYRNE is a native of southeastern Pennsylvania and a transplant to Tucson, Arizona. Somewhere in between, she received her MFA in creative writing from the University of Wisconsin-Madison. Her work has been published in *West Branch, The Journal, Hayden's Ferry Review,* and elsewhere.

DANNI QUINTOS is a Kentuckian and an Affrilachian Poet. Her poems have appeared in *Pluck!, Still,* and *Blood Lotus.* She is an MFA candidate in poetry at Indiana University in Bloomington.

SAM SAX is a 2015 NEA Creative Writing Fellow and a Poetry Fellow at The Michener Center for Writers where he serves as the editor-in-chief of *Bat City*

Review. He's the author of the chapbooks *A Guide to Undressing Your Monsters* (Button Poetry, 2014), *sad boy / detective* (Winner of the Black Lawrence's 2014 Black River Chapbook Prize) and *All The Rage* (SRP, 2016). His poems are forthcoming in *Beloit Poetry Journal, Boston Review, Pleiades, POETRY,* and other journals. He's a founding member of the writing collective Sad Boy Supper Club.

Originally from Atlanta, STEPHANIE ELLIS SCHLAIFER is a poet and installation artist in St. Louis. She has an MFA from the Iowa Writers' Workshop, and her poems have appeared in *AGNI, Denver Quarterly, LIT, Colorado Review, Fence,* and elsewhere. She is the author of the chapbook *Strangers with a Lifeboat,* illustrated by Jeff Pike. Her first full-length book, *Cleavemark,* is forthcoming from BOAAT Press in 2016. Schlaifer is a compulsive baker and is also very handy with a pitchfork.

EMILY SKAJA grew up next to a cemetery in northern Illinois. Her poems have been published by *Blackbird, Black Warrior Review, Devil's Lake, Gulf Coast, Indiana Review, The Journal, Linebreak, Mid-American Review, PANK, The Pinch, Pleiades, Southern Indiana Review,* and *Vinyl.* Emily was the winner of the 2015 *Gulf Coast* Poetry Prize and the runner-up for the 2014 *Black Warrior Review* Poetry Contest. She was also the recipient of the Russell Prize for emerging poets, an Academy of American Poets prize, and a 2015 AWP Intro Award. Emily is a recent graduate of the Purdue University MFA Program and lives in Ohio, where she is pursuing a PhD in poetry at the University of Cincinnati.

ANALICIA SOTELO holds an MFA from the University of Houston. Her poems have appeared in *The Antioch Review, The Indiana Review, West Branch, Subtropics, Waxwing,* and elsewhere. She is the recipient of a fellowship from the Ithaca Image-Text Workshop, out of which a collaborative book is forthcoming from ITI Press at Ithaca College.

DAVID THACKER is a PhD candidate in poetry at Florida State University and holds an MFA in poetry from the University of Idaho. A recipient of the Fredrick Manfred Award from the Western Literature Association, his poems have appeared in *Ploughshares, Subtropics, The Massachusetts Review,* and elsewhere.

EMILY VIZZO is a San Diego poet, journalist, and educator whose work has appeared in *FIELD, The Journal, North American Review, Blackbird, jubilat,* and *The Normal School.* A San Diego Area Writing Project Fellow, Emily served as assistant managing editor at *Drunken Boat* and as a VIDA counter. She currently volunteers with *Hunger Mountain* and *Poetry International,* offering free poetry workshops in underserved communities. Her essay "A Personal History of Dirt" was noted in *Best American Essays 2013.* She completed her MFA at Vermont College of Fine Arts, teaches yoga at the University of San Diego, and teaches both creative writing and journalism at the University of California, San Diego Extension. In 2015, she was a James Merrill Poetry Fellow at Vermont Studio Center.

CLAIRE WAHMANHOLM's poems most recently appear in *32 Poems, The Boiler, Waxwing,* and *Unsplendid,* and are forthcoming from *Handsome, Tinderbox Poetry Journal, The Journal, Parcel, The Kenyon Review Online, BOAAT, Sugared Water,* and *Third Coast.* She is a PhD student at the University of Utah, where she co-edits *Quarterly West.*

KARA KAI WANG is a graduate of the University of Oregon MFA's program. She is currently a first year medical student at the University of California, San Francisco.

AMY WOOLARD is a writer and public policy attorney working on foster care, juvenile justice, poverty, and homelessness issues in Virginia. She is a graduate of the Iowa Writers' Workshop and the University of Virginia School of Law.

Her poems have appeared in the *Virginia Quarterly Review, Ploughshares, Gulf Coast, Court Green, Fence, Indiana Review,* and *Best New Poets 2013,* among others, while her essays have run on *Slate, Pacific Standard, The Rumpus, Indiewire,* and elsewhere. She lives in Charlottesville, Virginia.

Nikki Zielinski's poems appear in such publications as *The Cincinnati Review, Vinyl, Southern Humanities Review, Sou'wester, Bellingham Review, PANK, Birmingham Poetry Review,* and others. Since completing her MFA in poetry at the University of Oregon, she has received fellowships from Djerassi, the Sewanee Writers' Conference, the Vermont Studio Center, the Bridport Arts Centre, and elsewhere, as well as an Ohio Arts Council Individual Excellence Award and Pushcart and Forward Prize nominations. A freelance editor in the sciences, she lives in Cleveland.

Acknowledgments

Mary Angelino's "Dinner at Nonna's" is forthcoming in *Sugar House Review*.

Jessica Bixel's "Lullaby for a Changeling" was previously published in *Handsome*.

Ian Burnette's "Harvests" was previously published in *The Adroit Journal*.

Laura Bylenok's "Infinite Regress" was previously published in *Pleiades*.

J. Jerome Cruz's "Saudades" was previously published in *New Delta Review*.

Jaydn DeWald's "Desire Lines" was previously published in *The Carolina Quarterly*.

Lisa Dordal's "Pretty Moon" was previously published in *Rove Poetry*.

Cody Ernst's "Come Up" was previously published in *Bayou Magazine*.

J.P. Grasser's "Well" was previously published in *Ecotone*.

Alysia Nicole Harris's "Crow's Sugar" was previously published in *Solstice Literary Magazine*.

Michael Derrick Hudson's "The Garden of Eden and the Trilobite" was previously published in *Boulevard*.

Trevor Ketner's "Gunshot Shards of Tiny's Steel Stars" was previously published in *The Sycamore Review*.

Ashley Keyser's "Land of Flowers" was previously published in *Passages North*.

Edgar Kunz's "My Father at 49, Working the Night Shift at B&R Diesel" was previously published in *Indiana Review*.

Eduardo Martinez-Leyva's "Confirmation" was previously published in *Apogee Journal*.

J.G. McClure's "Ars Poetica" was previously published in *Fourteen Hills*.

Elizabeth Metzger's "Not Spring" was previously published in *Tupelo Quarterly*.

Lena Moses-Schmitt's "The Gate" was previously published in *Devil's Lake*.

Jessica Nordell's "Girl, Running" is forthcoming in *Radar Poetry*.

sam sax's "gay boys and the bridges who love them" was previously published in *Drunken Boat*.

Emily Skaja's "Four Hawks" was previously published in *The Pinch*.

Analicia Sotelo's "I'm Trying to Write a Poem About a Virgin and It's Awful" was previously published in *The Antioch Review*.

David Thacker's "A Fetus Dreams Her Father's Brain Is a Tenement" was previously published in *Mid-American Review*.

Claire Wahmanholm's "Fallow" was previously published in *32 Poems*.

Amy Woolard's "A Place Where There Isn't Any Trouble" was previously published in *Court Green*.

Participating Magazines

32 Poems
32poems.com

AGNI Magazine
bu.edu/agni

Alligator Juniper
alligatorjuniper.org

Antioch Review
antiochreview.org

Apple Valley Review
applevalleyreview.com

apt
howapt.com

Arsenic Lobster Poetry Journal
arseniclobster.magere.com

Arts & Letters
artsandletters.gcsu.edu

Asheville Poetry Review
ashevillepoetryreview.com

B O D Y
bodyliterature.com

Beloit Poetry Journal
bpj.org

Birmingham Poetry Review
uab.edu/cas/englishpublications/
birmingham-poetry-review

Black Tongue Review
blacktonguereview.com

Blackbird
blackbird.vcu.edu

The Boiler
theboilerjournal.com

BOOTH
booth.butler.edu

Boston Review
bostonreview.net

cahoodaloodaling
cahoodaloodaling.com

Carbon Culture Review
carbonculturereview.com

The Carolina Quarterly
thecarolinaquarterly.com

Carve Magazine
carvezine.com

Cave Wall
cavewallpress.com

Cheat River Review
cheatriverreview.com

The Cincinnati Review
cincinnatireview.com

The Collagist
thecollagist.com

The Common
thecommononline.org

Crazyhorse
crazyhorse.cofc.edu

The Cumberland River Review
crr.trevecca.edu

Dappled Things
dappledthings.org

EVENT
eventmagazine.ca

Fjords Review
fjordsreview.com

Fogged Clarity
foggedclarity.com

Free State Review
freestatereview.com

The Georgia Review
thegeorgiareview.com

Gingerbread House
gingerbreadhouselitmag.com

Guernica Magazine
guernicamag.com

Hamilton Arts & Letters
HALmagazine.com

Harvard Review
harvardreview.org

Hayden's Ferry Review
haydensferryreview.blogspot.com

Image: Art, Faith, Mystery
imagejournal.org

The Iowa Review
iowareview.org

The Journal
thejournalmag.org

Juked
juked.com

Kenyon Review
kenyonreview.org

The Lascaux Review
lascauxreview.com

The Los Angeles Review
losangelesreview.org

Lunch Ticket
lunchticket.org

The Manhattan Review
themanhattanreview.com

Melancholy Hyperbole
melancholyhyperbole.com

Memorious: a journal of new
verse & fiction
memorious.org

Menacing Hedge
menacinghedge.com

Michigan Quarterly Review
michiganquarterlyreview.com

Muzzle Magazine
muzzlemagazine.com

Naugatuck River Review
naugatuckriverreview.com

New England Review
nereview.com

One Throne Magazine
onethrone.com

The Paris-American
theparisamerican.com

Pinwheel
pinwheeljournal.com

Pleiades
ucmo.edu/pleiades

Ploughshares
pshares.org

The Poet's Billow
thepoetsbillow.org

POETRY
poetrymagazine.org

PRISM international
prismmagazine.ca

Puerto del Sol
puertodelsol.org

Quarterly West
quarterlywest.com

Raleigh Review
RaleighReview.org

Rattle
rattle.com

The Rialto
therialto.co.uk

River Styx Magazine
riverstyx.org

Room Magazine
roommagazine.com

Ruminate Magazine
ruminatemagazine.com

Salamander
salamandermag.org

The Southeast Review
southeastreview.org

Southern Humanities Review
southernhumanitiesreview.com

Southern Indiana Review
southernindianareview.org

The Southern Review
thesouthernreview.org

Spillway
spillway.org

St. Petersburg Review
stpetersburgreview.com

Stirring: A Literary Collection
sundresspublications.com/stirring

Subtropics
subtropics.english.ufl.edu

Sugar House Review
sugarhousereview.com

Swarm
swarmlit.com

Tahoma Literary Review
tahomaliteraryreview.com

The Adroit Journal
theadroitjournal.org

The Believer
believermag.com

The Bitter Oleander
bitteroleander.com

Thrush Poetry Journal
thrushpoetryjournal.com

Toe Good Poetry
toegoodpoetry.com

Unsplendid
unsplendid.com

Up the Staircase Quarterly
upthestaircase.org

Verse Wisconsin
versewisconsin.org

Virginia Quarterly Review
vqronline.org

Waccamaw
waccamawjournal.com

Washington Square Review
washingtonsquarereview.com

Water-Stone Review
waterstonereview.com

Willow Springs
willowsprings.ewu.edu

Winter Tangerine Review
wintertangerine.com

Zymbol
zymbol.org

Participating Writing Programs

92Y Unterberg Poetry Center Writing Program
New York, NY
92y.org/WritingProgram

American University MFA Program in Creative Writing
Washington, DC
american.edu/cas/literature/mfa

Auburn University Creative Writing Program
Auburn, AL
cla.auburn.edu/english/graduate-studies/ma/concentration-in-creative-writing

Chapman University MFA Program in Creative Writing
Orange, CA
chapman.edu/wilkinson/graduate-studies/creative-writing-mfa.aspx

Columbia University MFA Program in Creative Writing
New York, NY
arts.columbia.edu/writing/about-mfa-program

Converse College Low Residency MFA
Spartanburg, SC
converse.edu/mfa

Fine Arts Work Center
Provincetown, MA
fawc.org

Florida International University Creative Writing Program
North Miami, FL
english.fiu.edu/creative-writing

The Florida State University Creative Writing Program
Tallahassee, FL
english.fsu.edu/crw

George Mason University Creative Writing Program
Fairfax, VA
creativewriting.gmu.edu

Hamline University Creative Writing Programs
St. Paul, MN
hamline.edu/cla/mfa

Hollins University Jackson Center for Creative Writing
Roanoke, VA
sites.google.com/site/hollinsmfa

Hunter College MFA Program
New York City, NY
hunter.cuny.edu/creativewriting

Iowa Writers' Workshop
Iowa City, IA
writersworkshop.uiowa.edu

Johns Hopkins University Writing Seminars
Baltimore, MD
writingseminars.jhu.edu

Minnesota State University, Mankato MFA Program in Creative Writing
Mankato, MN
english.mnsu.edu/cw

Murray State University MFA in Creative Writing
Murray, KY
murraystate.edu/Academics/
CollegesDepartments/
CollegeOfHumanitiesAndFineArts/
EnglishAndPhilosophy/GraduatePrograms/
MFACreativeWriting.aspx

New Mexico State University MFA in Creative Writing
Las Cruces, NM
english.nmsu.edu/graduate-programs/
m-f-a-creative-writing

The New School Writing Program
New York, NY
newschool.edu/public-engagement/
mfa-creative-writing

New York University Creative Writing Program
New York, NY
cwp.as.nyu.edu

North Carolina State University MFA in Creative Writing Program
Raleigh, NC
english.chass.ncsu.edu/graduate/mfa

Northwestern University School of Professional Studies MA/MFA in Creative Writing
Evanston, IL
sps.northwestern.edu/program-areas/
graduate/creative-writing

The Ohio State University Creative Writing Program
Columbus, OH
english.osu.edu/
creative-writing-ohio-state-university

Ohio University MA and PhD in Creative Writing
Athens, OH
english.ohiou.edu/cw

Oregon State University-Cascades Low-Residency MFA in Creative Writing
Bend, OR
osucascades.edu/academics/mfa

Pacific University MFA in Writing Program
Portland, OR
pacificu.edu/as/mfa

San Diego State University Creative Writing Program
San Diego, CA
mfa.sdsu.edu

Sarah Lawrence College Graduate Writing Program
Bronxville, NY
sarahlawrence.edu/writing-mfa

Southeast Missouri State University Department of English
Cape Girardeau, MO
semo.edu/english

Southern Connecticut State University MFA
New Haven, CT
southernct.edu/academics/schools/arts/
departments/english/creativewriting/
graduate

Texas Tech University Creative Writing Program
Lubbock, TX
depts.ttu.edu/english/cw

University of Arkansas Programs in Creative Writing and Translation
Fayetteville, AR
mfa.uark.edu

University of Connecticut Creative Writing Program
Storrs, CT
creativewriting.uconn.edu

The University of Georgia Creative Writing Program
Athens, GA
english.uga.edu/grad/areas/creativewrit.
html

University of Idaho MFA Program in Creative Writing
Moscow, ID
uidaho.edu/class/english/graduate/
mfaincreativewriting

**University of Illinois at Chicago
Program for Writers**
Chicago, IL
engl.uic.edu/CW

**University of Kansas Graduate
Creative Writing Program**
Lawrence, KS
englishcw.ku.edu

**University of Massachusetts
Boston MFA Program in Creative
Writing**
Boston, MA
umb.edu/academics/cla/english/grad/
mfa

**University of Massachusetts MFA
for Poets and Writers**
Amherst, MA
umass.edu/english/MFA_home.htm

**University of Michigan Helen Zell
Writers' Program**
Ann Arbor, MI
lsa.umich.edu/writers

**University of Mississippi MFA
Program in English**
Oxford, MS
mfaenglish.olemiss.edu

**University of Missouri Program in
Creative Writing**
Columbia, MO
english.missouri.edu/
creative-writing.html

**University of Missouri–St. Louis
MFA in Creative Writing**
St. Louis, MO
umsl.edu/~mfa

**University of North Texas Creative
Writing Program**
Denton, TX
english.unt.edu

**University of Notre Dame Creative
Writing Program**
Notre Dame, IN
english.nd.edu/creative-writing

**University of Oregon Creative
Writing Program**
Eugene, OR
crwr.uoregon.edu

**University of South Florida MFA in
Creative Writing Program**
Tampa, FL
english.usf.edu/graduate/concentrations/
cw/degrees

University of Southern Mississippi Center for Writers
Hattiesburg, MS
usm.edu/english

University of Tennessee Creative Writing Program
Knoxville, TN
english.utk.edu/
creative-writing-program

University of Texas Michener Center for Writers
Austin, TX
utexas.edu/academic/mcw

The University of Utah Creative Writing Program
Salt Lake City, UT
english.utah.edu/graduate/masters-studies/
creative-writing-mfa.php

Vermont College of Fine Arts MFA Program in Writing
Montpelier, VT
vcfa.edu/writing

Virginia Tech MFA Program in Creative Writing
Blacksburg, VA
graduate.english.vt.edu/MFA

West Virginia University MFA Program in Creative Writing
Morgantown, WV
creativewriting.wvu.edu

Western Michigan University Creative Writing Program
Kalamazoo, MI
wmich.edu/english

Whidbey Writers Workshop MFA, a Program of the Northwest Institute of Literary Arts
Langley, WA
nila.edu/mfa

TRACY K. SMITH is the author of the memoir *Ordinary Light* and three books of poetry: *Life on Mars*, which received the 2012 Pulitzer Prize; *Duende*, recipient of the 2006 James Laughlin Award, and *The Body's Question*, which won the 2002 Cave Canem Poetry Prize. Smith is also the recipient of the Academy of American Poets Fellowship, a Rona Jaffe Award and a Whiting Award. She was the Literature protégé in the 2009–2011 cycle of the Rolex Mentor and Protégé Arts Initiative.

JAZZY DANZIGER is the author of *Darkroom* (University of Wisconsin Press, 2012), which won the Brittingham Prize in Poetry, and has served as series editor for *Best New Poets* since 2011. She lives and works in St. Louis, Missouri and can be visited online at jazzydanziger.com.